P9-DWI-430

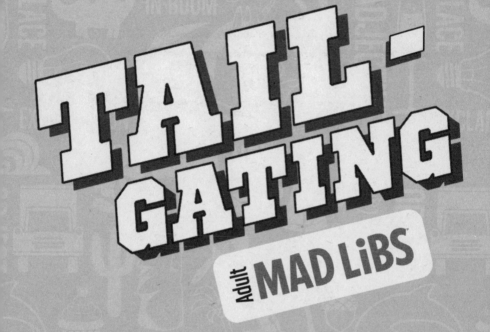

TAIL-GATING

Adult MAD LiBS

MAD LIBS
An imprint of Penguin Random House LLC, New York

Mad Libs format and text copyright © 2013, 2019 by Penguin Random House LLC. All rights reserved.

Concept created by Roger Price & Leonard Stern

Cover photographs: Thinkstock

Adult Mad Libs: Tailgating Mad Libs published in 2019 by Mad Libs,
an imprint of Penguin Random House LLC, New York.
Printed in the USA.

Visit us online at www.penguinrandomhouse.com.

Penguin supports copyright. Copyright fuels creativity, encourages diverse voices, promotes free speech, and creates a vibrant culture. Thank you for buying an authorized edition of this book and for complying with copyright laws by not reproducing, scanning, or distributing any part of it in any form without permission. You are supporting writers and allowing Penguin to continue to publish books for every reader.

Adult Mad Libs: Tailgating Mad Libs ISBN 9780593095942
1 3 5 7 9 10 8 6 4 2

MAD LIBS and ADULT MAD LIBS are registered trademarks of Penguin Random House LLC.

Adult MAD LIBS

The world's greatest _tailgate_ game

Pigskin Party Mad Libs

by Laura Marchesani & Zenaides A. Medina Jr.

MAD LIBS® is a game for people who don't like games! It can be played by one, two, three, four, or forty.

• RIDICULOUSLY SIMPLE DIRECTIONS

In this book, you'll find stories containing blank spaces where words are left out. One player, the READER, selects one of the stories. The READER shouldn't tell anyone what the story is about. Instead, the READER should ask the other players, the WRITERS, to give words to fill in the blank spaces in the story.

• TO PLAY

The READER asks each WRITER in turn to call out words—adjectives or nouns or whatever the spaces call for—and uses them to fill in the blank spaces in the story. The result is your very own MAD LIBS®! Then, when the READER reads the completed MAD LIBS® to the other players, they will discover they have written a story that is fantastic, screamingly funny, shocking, silly, crazy—or just plain dumb—depending on the words each WRITER called out.

• EXAMPLE (*Before* and *After*)

"_____ !" he said _____
         EXCLAMATION   ADVERB

as he jumped into his convertible _____ and
                                                   NOUN

drove off with his _____ wife.
                            ADJECTIVE

"_____*Ouch*_____ !" he said _____*stupidly*_____
         EXCLAMATION   ADVERB

as he jumped into his convertible _____*cat*_____ and
                                                   NOUN

drove off with his _____*brave*_____ wife.
                            ADJECTIVE

In case you have forgotten what adjectives, adverbs, nouns, and verbs are, here is a quick review:

An **ADJECTIVE** describes something or somebody. *Lumpy, soft, ugly, messy,* and *short* are adjectives.

An **ADVERB** tells how something is done. It modifies a verb and usually ends in "ly." *Modestly, stupidly, greedily,* and *carefully* are adverbs.

A **NOUN** is the name of a person, place, or thing. *Sidewalk, umbrella, bridle, bathtub,* and *nose* are nouns.

A **VERB** is an action word. *Run, pitch, jump,* and *swim* are verbs. Put the verbs in past tense if the directions say **PAST TENSE**. *Ran, pitched, jumped,* and *swam* are verbs in the past tense.

When we ask for **A PLACE**, we mean any sort of place: a country or city (*Spain, Cleveland*) or a room (*bathroom, kitchen*).

An **EXCLAMATION** or **SILLY WORD** is any sort of funny sound, gasp, grunt, or outcry, like *Wow!, Ouch!, Whomp!, Ick!,* and *Gadzooks!*

When we ask for specific words, like a **NUMBER**, a **COLOR**, an **ANIMAL**, or a **PART OF THE BODY**, we mean a word that is one of those things, like *seven, blue, horse,* or *head*.

When we ask for a **PLURAL**, it means more than one. For example, *cat* pluralized is *cats*.

Adult MAD LiBS

FOOTBALL FOR DUMMIES

The world's greatest _tailgate_ game

MAD LIBS® is fun to play with friends, but you can also play it by yourself! To begin with, DO NOT look at the story on the page below. Fill in the blanks on this page with the words called for. Then, using the words you have selected, fill in the blank spaces in the story. Now you've created your own hilarious MAD LIBS® game!

ADJECTIVE _____

VERB _____

PLURAL NOUN _____

NOUN _____

VERB _____

NOUN _____

NOUN _____

NUMBER _____

NOUN _____

NOUN _____

NUMBER _____

NOUN _____

PLURAL NOUN _____

NUMBER _____

NOUN _____

VERB _____

PLURAL NOUN _____

NOUN _____

Whether you're a _____ fan of the game, or just trying to
ADJECTIVE

_____ up on your football terminology, here's a list of football
VERB

_____ everyone should know:
PLURAL NOUN

- **Kickoff:** the beginning of each _____. Also occurs after a
NOUN

  team scores a/an _____ -down.
VERB

- **Touchback:** when a receiver catches the _____ and kneels
NOUN

  in the end _____. The ball is automatically moved to the
NOUN

  _____ -yard line.
NUMBER

- **Touchdown:** results when one team runs the _____ into the
NOUN

  other team's end _____. It is worth _____ points.
NOUN NUMBER

- **Field goal:** occurs when the _____ is kicked through the
NOUN

  _____. It is worth _____ points.
PLURAL NOUN NUMBER

- **Interception:** when a defensive _____ catches a forward
NOUN

  pass. He can _____ with the ball until he is tackled, pushed
VERB

  out of _____, or scores a touch- _____.
PLURAL NOUN NOUN

From ADULT MAD LIBS®: Pigskin Party Mad Libs • Copyright © 2013 by Penguin Random House LLC.

The world's greatest *tailgate* game

MAD LIBS® is fun to play with friends, but you can also play it by yourself! To begin with, DO NOT look at the story on the page below. Fill in the blanks on this page with the words called for. Then, using the words you have selected, fill in the blank spaces in the story. Now you've created your own hilarious MAD LIBS® game!

VERB ENDING IN "ING" _____

PERSON IN ROOM _____

PART OF THE BODY _____

ADJECTIVE _____

NUMBER _____

PLURAL NOUN _____

A PLACE _____

NOUN _____

PLURAL NOUN _____

NOUN _____

ADJECTIVE _____

VERB _____

NUMBER _____

NOUN _____

ADJECTIVE _____

ADJECTIVE _____

ADJECTIVE _____

VERB _____

COLOR _____

PLURAL NOUN _____

Adult MAD LiBS   FOOTBALL FOODIE

The world's greatest *tailgate* game

Are you _____ the big game at your friend _____'s house?

VERB ENDING IN "ING" ... PERSON IN ROOM

Don't show up empty-_____-ed! It would be _____

PART OF THE BODY ... ADJECTIVE

to swing by the local 7-_____ and grab a case of _____,

NUMBER ... PLURAL NOUN

but actually spending time in (the) _____ and cooking

A PLACE

a/an _____ will really impress your _____. Here's a/an

NOUN ... PLURAL NOUN

_____-proof recipe that even the most _____ cooks will

NOUN ... ADJECTIVE

be able to _____.

VERB

_____-Layer Taco Dip

NUMBER

Mix _____ seasoning and _____ beans and spread in the

NOUN ... ADJECTIVE

bottom of a/an _____ serving dish. Mix _____ cream

ADJECTIVE ... ADJECTIVE

with cream cheese and _____ on top of the beans. Top with

VERB

salsa, _____ peppers, and cheddar cheese, and garnish with

COLOR

_____. Serve hot!

PLURAL NOUN

From ADULT MAD LIBS®: Pigskin Party Mad Libs • Copyright © 2013 by Penguin Random House LLC.

MAD LIBS® is fun to play with friends, but you can also play it by yourself! To begin with, DO NOT look at the story on the page below. Fill in the blanks on this page with the words called for. Then, using the words you have selected, fill in the blank spaces in the story. Now you've created your own hilarious MAD LIBS® game!

SILLY WORD _____

ADJECTIVE _____

NOUN _____

NUMBER _____

A PLACE _____

ADJECTIVE _____

ARTICLE OF CLOTHING _____

ADJECTIVE _____

PLURAL NOUN _____

NOUN _____

NOUN _____

PART OF THE BODY (PLURAL) _____

NOUN _____

PART OF THE BODY (PLURAL) _____

PLURAL NOUN _____

ADJECTIVE _____

VERB ENDING IN "ING" _____

ADVERB _____

CELEBRITY _____

PERSON IN ROOM _____

_____! It's the moment you've been waiting for! Your manager
  SILLY WORD

just called to tell you that you will be performing at the halftime

show of this year's _____ Bowl. If you want your _____
                        ADJECTIVE   NOUN

to be applauded by _____ fans all around (the) _____,
                       NUMBER   A PLACE

here are a few _____ tips to follow:
                   ADJECTIVE

DO wear your best _____—the more _____, the better!
                      ARTICLE OF CLOTHING   ADJECTIVE

DON'T forget to button any _____ or zip up your
                                   PLURAL NOUN

_____. A wardrobe malfunction could ruin your _____!
  NOUN   NOUN

DO show off your best assets, like your long _____ or
                                              PART OF THE BODY (PLURAL)

voluptuous _____.
              NOUN

DON'T forget to shave your _____ or trim your
                                  PART OF THE BODY (PLURAL)

_____. Remember—most TVs are _____-definition now!
  PLURAL NOUN   ADJECTIVE

DO memorize your lyrics and practice _____ in key.
                                          VERB ENDING IN "ING"

DON'T sing so _____ that you get booed offstage like
                     ADVERB

_____'s little sister, _____ Simpson!
  CELEBRITY   PERSON IN ROOM

From ADULT MAD LIBS®: Pigskin Party Mad Libs • Copyright © 2013 by Penguin Random House LLC.

MAD LIBS® is fun to play with friends, but you can also play it by yourself! To begin with, DO NOT look at the story on the page below. Fill in the blanks on this page with the words called for. Then, using the words you have selected, fill in the blank spaces in the story. Now you've created your own hilarious MAD LIBS® game!

NOUN _____

ADJECTIVE _____

PERSON IN ROOM _____

NOUN _____

ADJECTIVE _____

ADJECTIVE _____

VERB _____

ADJECTIVE _____

A PLACE _____

PERSON IN ROOM _____

NOUN _____

ADJECTIVE _____

ADJECTIVE _____

PART OF THE BODY (PLURAL) _____

ADJECTIVE _____

PLURAL NOUN _____

PART OF THE BODY _____

COLOR _____

NOUN _____

TYPE OF FOOD (PLURAL) _____

There are a/an _____-load of _____ movies about the
            NOUN   ADJECTIVE

game of football. Here are a few to help you get your football fix:

- _____'s _Song_: A/An _____-jerker about
    PERSON IN ROOM   NOUN

  two teammates who become _____ friends. It's a/an
                                  ADJECTIVE

  _____ idea to _____ this one alone.
    ADJECTIVE   VERB

- _Friday Night Lights_: A/An _____ look at a small town in
                        ADJECTIVE

  (the) _____ obsessed with football.
      A PLACE

- _We Are_ _____: Break out a/an _____ of tissues!
      PERSON IN ROOM   NOUN

  In this _____ movie, a university rallies together after
          ADJECTIVE

  a plane crash. The story will melt even the most _____
                                       ADJECTIVE

  of _____ .
    PART OF THE BODY (PLURAL)

- _____ _Giants_: A family comedy about two rival football
    ADJECTIVE

  _____ , starring comedian Rick Moranis and former
    PLURAL NOUN

  _____-throb Devon Sawa.
    PART OF THE BODY

- _Varsity_ _____s: A/An _____ famous for a scene with
          COLOR   NOUN

  a bikini made out of _____ .
             TYPE OF FOOD (PLURAL)

From ADULT MAD LIBS®: Pigskin Party Mad Libs • Copyright © 2013 by Penguin Random House LLC.

MAD LIBS® is fun to play with friends, but you can also play it by yourself! To begin with, DO NOT look at the story on the page below. Fill in the blanks on this page with the words called for. Then, using the words you have selected, fill in the blank spaces in the story. Now you've created your own hilarious MAD LIBS® game!

NOUN _____

NUMBER _____

NOUN _____

PLURAL NOUN _____

ADVERB _____

NOUN _____

ADJECTIVE _____

NOUN _____

PLURAL NOUN _____

NUMBER _____

NOUN _____

NUMBER _____

PLURAL NOUN _____

NOUN _____

VERB (PAST TENSE) _____

ADJECTIVE _____

NOUN _____

EXCLAMATION _____

ARTICLE OF CLOTHING _____

VERB _____

The world's greatest *tailgate* game

The Super Bowl is the annual _____ played by _____
                                    NOUN   NUMBER

teams to decide the champion of the NFL, or National _____
                                                            NOUN

League. The first Super Bowl was played in 1967 between the Green

Bay _____ and the Kansas City Chiefs. Now the Super Bowl
       PLURAL NOUN

is _____ the most-watched _____ of the year, thanks
      ADVERB   NOUN

in part to the _____ commercials and over-the- _____
                    ADJECTIVE   NOUN

halftime performances. The Pittsburgh _____ have won
                                            PLURAL NOUN

_____ Super Bowls, the most of any _____ , followed
   NUMBER   NOUN

by the Dallas Cowboys and the San Francisco _____ -ers, with
                                                  NUMBER

five _____ apiece. The Super Bowl is played in a different
        PLURAL NOUN

_____ every year, and no team has ever _____ in its
   NOUN   VERB (PAST TENSE)

own stadium! The _____ Bowl is like a national holiday in
                      ADJECTIVE

the United States and is the second-largest day for _____
                                                          NOUN

consumption, after Thanksgiving. _____ ! Better break out
                                      EXCLAMATION

your stretchy _____ —it's time to _____ some football!
                 ARTICLE OF CLOTHING   VERB

From ADULT MAD LIBS®: Pigskin Party Mad Libs • Copyright © 2013 by Penguin Random House LLC.

MAD LIBS® is fun to play with friends, but you can also play it by yourself! To begin with, DO NOT look at the story on the page below. Fill in the blanks on this page with the words called for. Then, using the words you have selected, fill in the blank spaces in the story. Now you've created your own hilarious MAD LIBS® game!

ADJECTIVE _____

PERSON IN ROOM _____

NOUN _____

ADJECTIVE _____

ADJECTIVE _____

ADJECTIVE _____

PLURAL NOUN _____

PLURAL NOUN _____

ADJECTIVE _____

PERSON IN ROOM _____

A PLACE _____

PART OF THE BODY (PLURAL) _____

NOUN _____

PLURAL NOUN _____

ADJECTIVE _____

TYPE OF LIQUID _____

ADJECTIVE _____

ADJECTIVE _____

PART OF THE BODY (PLURAL) _____

VERB _____

Adult MAD LiBS
PARTY LIKE IT'S SUPER BOWL SUNDAY

The world's greatest _tailgate_ game

Do you want to throw the best Super Bowl party on the block?

Want to show up your _____ neighbor _____ and have
                         ADJECTIVE   PERSON IN ROOM

something to brag about at the _____-cooler on Monday? Here
                                      NOUN

are the secrets to Super Bowl party success:

1. Buy a new _____-screen TV. Even if you think your TV is
                  ADJECTIVE

   big, it's not _____ enough!
                    ADJECTIVE

2. Invite only the most _____ _____ in the
                            ADJECTIVE   PLURAL NOUN

   neighborhood. That means your friends with the best

   _____ and not your _____ cousin _____ .
    PLURAL NOUN   ADJECTIVE   PERSON IN ROOM

3. Send the spouse and kids off to (the) _____ . You don't
                                              A PLACE

   want anyone nagging you to keep your _____ off the
                                         PART OF THE BODY (PLURAL)

   coffee table or to put a coaster under your _____ .
                                                     NOUN

4. Serve _____ and dip and _____ wings. Keep your
             PLURAL NOUN   ADJECTIVE

   fridge stocked with cans of _____ and avoid anything
                                 TYPE OF LIQUID

   _____ like Mike's _____ Lemonade.
    ADJECTIVE   ADJECTIVE

5. Put your _____ up and relax. And if you followed rule
             PART OF THE BODY (PLURAL)

   #3, it means your spouse isn't there to _____ at you!
                                                VERB

From ADULT MAD LIBS®: Pigskin Party Mad Libs • Copyright © 2013 by Penguin Random House LLC.

Adult MAD LiBS

SO YOUR WIFE HATES FOOTBALL?

The world's greatest *tailgate* game

MAD LIBS® is fun to play with friends, but you can also play it by yourself! To begin with, DO NOT look at the story on the page below. Fill in the blanks on this page with the words called for. Then, using the words you have selected, fill in the blank spaces in the story. Now you've created your own hilarious MAD LIBS® game!

PLURAL NOUN _____

ADJECTIVE _____

ADJECTIVE _____

NOUN _____

PLURAL NOUN _____

TYPE OF FOOD _____

PLURAL NOUN _____

VERB _____

NOUN _____

NOUN _____

VERB _____

ADJECTIVE _____

ADJECTIVE _____

PLURAL NOUN _____

COLOR _____

ADJECTIVE _____

NOUN _____

ADVERB _____

PART OF THE BODY (PLURAL) _____

Adult MAD LiBS

SO YOUR WIFE HATES FOOTBALL?

The world's greatest *tailgate* game

So you married the woman of your _____ , and everything

PLURAL NOUN

is _____ except for one _____ thing—she hates football!

ADJECTIVE · ADJECTIVE

What do you do? You could throw in the _____ and accept

NOUN

that from now on your Sundays will be spent shopping for

_____ or eating _____ toast at brunch. Or you could use

PLURAL NOUN · TYPE OF FOOD

your _____ of persuasion and try to convince her to love the

PLURAL NOUN

game you _____ so much! Start with the rules. She can't get

VERB

into the _____ if she doesn't know the difference between a/

NOUN

an _____ goal and a/an _____-down! Then go out and

NOUN · VERB

buy her a jersey from your _____ team. After all, everyone loves

ADJECTIVE

_____ clothes—even football _____! Bonus points if it's

ADJECTIVE · PLURAL NOUN

a special-edition _____ jersey. If all else fails, point out how

COLOR

_____ the players on the team are. She may not appreciate the

ADJECTIVE

excitement of the _____ , but she will _____ appreciate

NOUN · ADVERB

muscular _____!

PART OF THE BODY (PLURAL)

From ADULT MAD LIBS®: Pigskin Party Mad Libs • Copyright © 2013 by Penguin Random House LLC.

Adult MAD LiBS

DRESS TO IMPRESS

The world's greatest *tailgate* game

MAD LIBS® is fun to play with friends, but you can also play it by yourself! To begin with, DO NOT look at the story on the page below. Fill in the blanks on this page with the words called for. Then, using the words you have selected, fill in the blank spaces in the story. Now you've created your own hilarious MAD LIBS® game!

PERSON IN ROOM _____

NUMBER _____

EXCLAMATION _____

ADJECTIVE _____

NOUN _____

ADJECTIVE _____

VERB _____

NUMBER _____

LAST NAME _____

VERB _____

ADVERB _____

ADJECTIVE _____

PART OF THE BODY _____

PLURAL NOUN _____

A PLACE _____

ADJECTIVE _____

COLOR _____

ADJECTIVE _____

NUMBER _____

PLURAL NOUN _____

Adult MAD LiBS

DRESS TO IMPRESS

The world's greatest *tailgate* game

Your buddy _____ has somehow managed to score tickets

PERSON IN ROOM

to this season's biggest game. And—get this—the seats are in the

front row on the _____ -yard line. _____! And now

NUMBER .... EXCLAMATION

the _____ day is finally here, and you have no _____

ADJECTIVE .... NOUN

what to wear. Chances are, you'll make it onto TV, and you want to

look _____ when you do! Of course, you have to _____

ADJECTIVE .... VERB

your team's jersey, but which one? You have _____ of them!

NUMBER

Should you go with your _____ throwback jersey? Or is it

LAST NAME

better to _____ your brand-new, _____ -worn jersey

VERB .... ADVERB

of this season's _____ rookie? And should you paint your

ADJECTIVE

_____ or not? Face paint will show your support of the team,

PART OF THE BODY

but will your _____ watching at (the) _____ be able to

PLURAL NOUN .... A PLACE

recognize you? And what about accessories, like your _____ hat

ADJECTIVE

or _____ scarf? Being a fan sure is _____ sometimes. But

COLOR .... ADJECTIVE

being the number _____ fan? It takes a lot of _____!

NUMBER .... PLURAL NOUN

From ADULT MAD LIBS®: Pigskin Party Mad Libs • Copyright © 2013 by Penguin Random House LLC.

MAD LIBS® is fun to play with friends, but you can also play it by yourself! To begin with, DO NOT look at the story on the page below. Fill in the blanks on this page with the words called for. Then, using the words you have selected, fill in the blank spaces in the story. Now you've created your own hilarious MAD LIBS® game!

ADJECTIVE _____

NOUN _____

NOUN _____

VERB (PAST TENSE) _____

ADJECTIVE _____

ADJECTIVE _____

PART OF THE BODY _____

LETTER OF THE ALPHABET _____

ADJECTIVE _____

ADJECTIVE _____

PART OF THE BODY (PLURAL) _____

VERB ENDING IN "ING" _____

NOUN _____

ADJECTIVE _____

PART OF THE BODY (PLURAL) _____

NOUN _____

VERB _____

ARTICLE OF CLOTHING (PLURAL) _____

NOUN _____

One of the most _____ places to get a date is at a football game
_____ ADJECTIVE

or tailgate _____ ! For one thing, if someone's at the _____ ,
_____ NOUN _____ NOUN

it means that they love football as much as you do, so you'll never

get _____ at when you want to watch the _____ game.
VERB (PAST TENSE) _____ ADJECTIVE

Plus, who doesn't look super- _____ in football jerseys? Hubba
_____ ADJECTIVE

hubba! To win over their _____ , you're going to have to be on
PART OF THE BODY

your _____ game. Here are a few _____ lines to help you
LETTER OF THE ALPHABET _____ ADJECTIVE

pick up the most _____ -looking fan at the game:
_____ ADJECTIVE

• Are your _____ tired, because you've been _____
PART OF THE BODY (PLURAL) _____ VERB ENDING IN "ING"

through my mind all day long.

• I hope you know CPR, because you take my _____ away!
_____ NOUN

• Do you have a sunburn, or are you always this _____ ?
_____ ADJECTIVE

• Your _____ are the same color as my Porsche.
PART OF THE BODY (PLURAL)

• Was that a/an _____ -quake or did you just _____ my world?
_____ NOUN _____ VERB

• Are your _____ on sale? Because if you were in my
ARTICLE OF CLOTHING (PLURAL)

_____ , they'd be 100 percent off!
NOUN

From ADULT MAD LIBS®: Pigskin Party Mad Libs • Copyright © 2013 by Penguin Random House LLC.

The world's greatest *tailgate* game

MAD LIBS® is fun to play with friends, but you can also play it by yourself! To begin with, DO NOT look at the story on the page below. Fill in the blanks on this page with the words called for. Then, using the words you have selected, fill in the blank spaces in the story. Now you've created your own hilarious MAD LIBS® game!

PLURAL NOUN _____

ADJECTIVE _____

ADJECTIVE _____

PART OF THE BODY _____

VERB _____

ADJECTIVE _____

PERSON IN ROOM _____

CELEBRITY _____

NUMBER _____

PLURAL NOUN _____

NOUN _____

NUMBER _____

ADJECTIVE _____

ANIMAL (PLURAL) _____

VERB _____

NUMBER _____

ADJECTIVE _____

NOUN _____

Quarterbacks are the _____ of every football team—everyone
_{PLURAL NOUN}

knows their names, even if they're only _____ fans. Their
_{ADJECTIVE}

jerseys are the most _____ sellers. And they're seen as
_{ADJECTIVE}

_____-throbs, no matter what they _____ like! Here are
_{PART OF THE BODY} _{VERB}

some of the most _____-known quarterbacks in history.
_{ADJECTIVE}

- _____ **Brady:** more famous for marrying his wife,
  _{PERSON IN ROOM}

  model _____ , than for the _____ championships
  _{CELEBRITY} _{NUMBER}

  he's won with the New England _____
  _{PLURAL NOUN}

- **Brett Favre:** once a beloved member of the Green Bay Packers,

  but after retiring and then rejoining the NFL as a New York

  _____ , he lost _____ fans
  _{NOUN} _{NUMBER}

- **Dan Marino:** a/an _____ quarterback for the Miami
  _{ADJECTIVE}

  _____ , but he was never able to _____ a Super Bowl
  _{ANIMAL (PLURAL)} _{VERB}

- **Joe Montana:** won _____ Super Bowls with the San
  _{NUMBER}

  Francisco 49ers and is famous for his _____ play known as
  _{ADJECTIVE}

  "The _____ "
  _{NOUN}

From ADULT MAD LIBS®: Pigskin Party Mad Libs • Copyright © 2013 by Penguin Random House LLC.

Adult MAD LiBS

SUNDAY EATS

The world's greatest *tailgate* game

MAD LIBS® is fun to play with friends, but you can also play it by yourself! To begin with, DO NOT look at the story on the page below. Fill in the blanks on this page with the words called for. Then, using the words you have selected, fill in the blank spaces in the story. Now you've created your own hilarious MAD LIBS® game!

PLURAL NOUN _____

NOUN _____

PLURAL NOUN _____

PLURAL NOUN _____

ADJECTIVE _____

NUMBER _____

ANIMAL _____

ADJECTIVE _____

NOUN _____

NOUN _____

PLURAL NOUN _____

ADJECTIVE _____

NUMBER _____

PLURAL NOUN _____

NOUN _____

ADJECTIVE _____

PLURAL NOUN _____

A PLACE _____

PLURAL NOUN _____

ADJECTIVE _____

Are you planning to have some _____ over for the game this
<small>PLURAL NOUN</small>

Sunday? Or perhaps you're meeting some friends at the stadium and

want to plan a/an _____ -gate party? Here's a menu that your
<small>NOUN</small>

_____ are sure to love. Start by serving _____ and dip.
<small>PLURAL NOUN</small>   <small>PLURAL NOUN</small>

_____ salsa, _____ -layer dip, and buffalo- _____
<small>ADJECTIVE</small>   <small>NUMBER</small>   <small>ANIMAL</small>

dip are always crowd-pleasers! If it's _____ outside, fire up
<small>ADJECTIVE</small>

the grill. Throw a couple _____ -burgers and hot dogs on the
<small>NOUN</small>

_____ , and serve with plenty of condiments like ketchup,
<small>NOUN</small>

mustard, and _____ . If it's too _____ to grill, order
<small>PLURAL NOUN</small>   <small>ADJECTIVE</small>

in _____ pizzas, a bucket of hot _____ , or a party-size
<small>NUMBER</small>   <small>PLURAL NOUN</small>

_____ . Dessert is _____ , but not necessary. Bake up a
<small>NOUN</small>   <small>ADJECTIVE</small>

sheet of _____ or pick up a cake from (the) _____ . And
<small>PLURAL NOUN</small>   <small>A PLACE</small>

no matter what you do, make sure you have plenty of _____ to
<small>PLURAL NOUN</small>

drink! It's always a party if everyone is _____ .
<small>ADJECTIVE</small>

From ADULT MAD LIBS*: Pigskin Party Mad Libs • Copyright © 2013 by Penguin Random House LLC.

The world's greatest _tailgate_ game

MAD LIBS® is fun to play with friends, but you can also play it by yourself! To begin with, DO NOT look at the story on the page below. Fill in the blanks on this page with the words called for. Then, using the words you have selected, fill in the blank spaces in the story. Now you've created your own hilarious MAD LIBS® game!

ADJECTIVE _____

ADJECTIVE _____

A PLACE _____

PLURAL NOUN _____

TYPE OF LIQUID _____

ADJECTIVE _____

ADJECTIVE _____

NOUN _____

PLURAL NOUN _____

NUMBER _____

VERB _____

PLURAL NOUN _____

PLURAL NOUN _____

NUMBER _____

ADJECTIVE _____

PART OF THE BODY (PLURAL) _____

NOUN _____

ADJECTIVE _____

TYPE OF LIQUID _____

VERB _____

VERB _____

Adult MAD LiBS · FUN AND GAMES

The world's greatest *tailgate* game

Tailgating is a rite of passage for _____ college students and football
                                    ADJECTIVE

fans everywhere. Sure, it's _____ just to sit in (the) _____
                             ADJECTIVE   A PLACE

outside the stadium and eat _____ hot off the grill and drink cans
                            PLURAL NOUN

of _____. But it can be a lot more _____ when games are
   TYPE OF LIQUID   ADJECTIVE

involved! Here are some of the most _____ tailgating games:
                                    ADJECTIVE

Cornhole, also known as _____-**bag toss** or **baggo**, is a game in
                            NOUN

which _____ take turns throwing bags at a raised platform. The
      PLURAL NOUN

first player to reach _____ wins.
                      NUMBER

Ladder Golf or **Football** _____ involves throwing _____
                                VERB   PLURAL NOUN

attached to the ends of cords at horizontal _____ in order to
                                            PLURAL NOUN

score points.

Polish Horseshoes is played between _____ teams of people
                                        NUMBER

using a Frisbee and two _____ bottles. Players must hold a drink
                        ADJECTIVE

in their _____ at all times during the _____.
         PART OF THE BODY (PLURAL)   NOUN

Beer pong is a/an _____ game that involves throwing Ping-
                      ADJECTIVE

Pong balls at cups of _____. When you _____ a ball into
                      TYPE OF LIQUID   VERB

your opponent's cup, he has to _____!
                               VERB

From ADULT MAD LIBS®: Pigskin Party Mad Libs • Copyright © 2013 by Penguin Random House LLC.

MAD LIBS® is fun to play with friends, but you can also play it by yourself! To begin with, DO NOT look at the story on the page below. Fill in the blanks on this page with the words called for. Then, using the words you have selected, fill in the blank spaces in the story. Now you've created your own hilarious MAD LIBS® game!

PART OF THE BODY (PLURAL) _____

ADJECTIVE _____

ADJECTIVE _____

ADJECTIVE _____

NOUN _____

ADJECTIVE _____

ANIMAL _____

PERSON IN ROOM _____

NUMBER_____

ADJECTIVE _____

ADJECTIVE _____

NOUN _____

ANIMAL _____

ADJECTIVE _____

NOUN _____

VERB ENDING IN "ING" _____

ADVERB _____

ADJECTIVE _____

VERB_____

NOUN _____

Both professional and college football teams have mascots to energize the

crowd and bring the fans to their _____ during _____

PART OF THE BODY (PLURAL)   ADJECTIVE

moments. Who is the most _____ mascot in all of football? It's

ADJECTIVE

hard to choose! Traveler is a/an _____ mascot for the USC Trojans.

ADJECTIVE

He isn't a/an _____ in a costume—he's a real, _____

NOUN   ADJECTIVE

_____! The Buffalo _____ s' mascot is a/an _____

ANIMAL   PERSON IN ROOM   NUMBER

-foot tall buffalo named Billy—and he looks like a character straight

out of the book *Where the* _____ *Things Are*! The first mascot

ADJECTIVE

was _____ Dan, a bull- _____ at Yale University. Swoop

ADJECTIVE   NOUN

is the Philadelphia Eagles' mascot. And—you guessed it—he's

a/an _____ . Believe it or not, Stanford University's mascot is

ANIMAL

a/an _____ tree. But this tree knows how to be the _____

ADJECTIVE   NOUN

of the party—in 2006, he was seen _____ out of a flask and

VERB ENDING IN "ING"

was _____ arrested. There are too many _____ mascots to

ADVERB   ADJECTIVE

_____ a favorite. But if I had to pick just one it would be Phil—the

VERB

character that you see on the front _____ of many Mad Libs books!

NOUN

From ADULT MAD LIBS®: Pigskin Party Mad Libs • Copyright © 2013 by Penguin Random House LLC.

Adult MAD LiBS — SUPER COMMERCIALS

The world's greatest *tailgate* game

MAD LIBS® is fun to play with friends, but you can also play it by yourself! To begin with, DO NOT look at the story on the page below. Fill in the blanks on this page with the words called for. Then, using the words you have selected, fill in the blank spaces in the story. Now you've created your own hilarious MAD LIBS® game!

NUMBER _____

SILLY WORD _____

VERB _____

ADJECTIVE _____

PART OF THE BODY _____

ADJECTIVE _____

PERSON IN ROOM _____

ADJECTIVE _____

ADJECTIVE _____

ADJECTIVE _____

PLURAL NOUN _____

ANIMAL _____

NOUN _____

ADJECTIVE _____

ANIMAL (PLURAL) _____

SILLY WORD _____

COLOR _____

NUMBER _____

PLURAL NOUN _____

A PLACE _____

ADJECTIVE _____

Adult MAD LiBS — SUPER COMMERCIALS

The world's greatest _tailgate_ game

Even though _____ people tune in to the Super Bowl every
NUMBER

year, many fans don't actually give a/an _____ about the
SILLY WORD

game! So why do they _____? For the commercials, of course!
VERB

The first _____ commercial was for _____ cleanser
ADJECTIVE   PART OF THE BODY

Noxzema. It aired in 1973 and starred Joe Namath and _____
ADJECTIVE

actress _____ Fawcett. Another famous commercial was
PERSON IN ROOM

for the _____ beverage Coca-Cola and featured "_____
ADJECTIVE   ADJECTIVE

Joe" Greene. In 1993 a/an _____ ad showed basketball
ADJECTIVE

_____ Michael Jordan and Larry _____ playing a
PLURAL NOUN   ANIMAL

game of _____ for a/an _____ Mac and french fries
NOUN   ADJECTIVE

from McDonald's. And don't forget the Budweiser _____,
ANIMAL (PLURAL)

the Volkswagen ad starring a young Darth _____, and
SILLY WORD

Betty _____ eating a Snickers. And of course, some of the
COLOR

most popular commercials over the past _____ years have
NUMBER

featured athletes and other _____ saying, "I'm going to (the)
PLURAL NOUN

_____!" What's your favorite Super Bowl commercial? It's too
A PLACE

_____ to choose just one!
ADJECTIVE

From ADULT MAD LIBS®: Pigskin Party Mad Libs • Copyright © 2013 by Penguin Random House LLC.

MAD LIBS® is fun to play with friends, but you can also play it by yourself! To begin with, DO NOT look at the story on the page below. Fill in the blanks on this page with the words called for. Then, using the words you have selected, fill in the blank spaces in the story. Now you've created your own hilarious MAD LIBS® game!

ADJECTIVE _____

VERB _____

NOUN _____

PERSON IN ROOM _____

VERB _____

NOUN _____

ADJECTIVE _____

ADJECTIVE _____

PART OF THE BODY _____

ADJECTIVE _____

VERB _____

NOUN _____

LETTER OF THE ALPHABET _____

PART OF THE BODY (PLURAL) _____

ADJECTIVE _____

ADJECTIVE _____

ANIMAL _____

VERB ENDING IN "ING" _____

There are many _____ traditions in college football:
          ADJECTIVE

- In Wisconsin, students _____ together in a/an
                                   VERB

  _____ called Camp _____ . After the third
  NOUN   PERSON IN ROOM

  quarter, they _____ to the song "Jump Around."
                 VERB

- Florida State fans are famous for their tomahawk _____ ,
                                        NOUN

  while their rivals at the University of Florida cheer their team with

  the _____ Gator Chomp.
       ADJECTIVE

- Texas Longhorn fans show their pride with a/an _____
                                ADJECTIVE

  _____ gesture and a/an _____ cheer—
  PART OF THE BODY   ADJECTIVE

  "_____ 'em!"
    VERB

- Nebraska _____-husker fans make a/an _____
          NOUN   LETTER OF THE ALPHABET

  symbol with their _____ during any _____
              PART OF THE BODY (PLURAL)   ADJECTIVE

  defensive play.

- Michigan State has a/an _____ halftime show starring
                 ADJECTIVE

  Zeke the Wonder _____ , a Frisbee-_____ dog.
           ANIMAL   VERB ENDING IN "ING"

From ADULT MAD LIBS®: Pigskin Party Mad Libs • Copyright © 2013 by Penguin Random House LLC.

MAD LIBS® is fun to play with friends, but you can also play it by yourself! To begin with, DO NOT look at the story on the page below. Fill in the blanks on this page with the words called for. Then, using the words you have selected, fill in the blank spaces in the story. Now you've created your own hilarious MAD LIBS® game!

VERB _____

A PLACE _____

PLURAL NOUN _____

PLURAL NOUN _____

ADJECTIVE _____

VERB _____

TYPE OF FOOD _____

ADJECTIVE _____

NOUN _____

PERSON IN ROOM _____

PLURAL NOUN _____

PLURAL NOUN _____

VERB _____

PLURAL NOUN _____

NUMBER _____

VERB _____

ADJECTIVE _____

NOUN _____

ADJECTIVE _____

VERB ENDING IN "ING" _____

There are many different ways to _____ tickets to a football

VERB

game. It used to be that you would go to (the) _____

A PLACE

and buy the _____ in person. But now, thanks to the

PLURAL NOUN

Internet, buying _____ is easier than ever! Log on to your

PLURAL NOUN

_____ team's website, find the best seats, and _____!

ADJECTIVE   VERB

It's as easy as _____ . But other websites may offer

TYPE OF FOOD

more _____ deals. Before you buy, check out sites like

ADJECTIVE

Stub-_____ .com or _____-slist.com to see if your

NOUN   PERSON IN ROOM

_____ are there, too. This is where _____ with

PLURAL NOUN   PLURAL NOUN

season tickets or extra tickets they can't _____ go to sell

VERB

their seats. Sometimes you can buy _____ for as little as

PLURAL NOUN

$ _____ ! But before you _____ , make sure it's not a

NUMBER   VERB

scam. Sometimes these deals seem too _____ to be true! You

ADJECTIVE

can always watch the _____ on your _____ -screen

NOUN   ADJECTIVE

television at home, but nothing beats _____ the game in

VERB ENDING IN "ING"

person!

From ADULT MAD LIBS®: Pigskin Party Mad Libs • Copyright © 2013 by Penguin Random House LLC.

MAD LiBS

MEMORABLE MATCHUPS

The world's greatest *tailgate* game

MAD LIBS® is fun to play with friends, but you can also play it by yourself! To begin with, DO NOT look at the story on the page below. Fill in the blanks on this page with the words called for. Then, using the words you have selected, fill in the blank spaces in the story. Now you've created your own hilarious MAD LIBS® game!

ADJECTIVE _____

PLURAL NOUN _____

ADJECTIVE _____

A PLACE _____

VERB _____

ANIMAL (PLURAL) _____

ADJECTIVE _____

PLURAL NOUN _____

NOUN _____

PLURAL NOUN _____

NOUN _____

ADJECTIVE _____

VERB _____

PERSON IN ROOM _____

ANIMAL (PLURAL) _____

NOUN _____

ADJECTIVE _____

CELEBRITY _____

PART OF THE BODY _____

Adult MAD LiBS

MEMORABLE MATCHUPS

The world's greatest *tailgate* game

The Super Bowl is the most _____ game of the year. There
ADJECTIVE

have been many memorable _____ over the years, but here are
PLURAL NOUN

a few of the most _____ :
ADJECTIVE

- **Super Bowl III:** The _____ Jets defeated the
A PLACE

  Baltimore Colts and became the first AFL team ever to

  _____ a Super Bowl. Joe Namath and the Jets were
VERB

  the under- _____ , but Joe guaranteed a victory for his
ANIMAL (PLURAL)

  team—and he was _____ !
ADJECTIVE

- **Super Bowl XVI:** The San Francisco _____ beat
PLURAL NOUN

  the Cincinnati Bengals, and it was Joe Montana's first Super

  _____ victory. The 49ers came from behind to beat the
NOUN

  Dallas _____ in the AFC Championship _____ , so
PLURAL NOUN   NOUN

  it was _____ that they managed to _____ again!
ADJECTIVE   VERB

- **Super Bowl XXXVIII:** _____ Brady and the New
PERSON IN ROOM

  England Patriots defeated the Carolina _____ by only a/an
ANIMAL (PLURAL)

  _____ goal! This was also the Super Bowl _____
NOUN   ADJECTIVE

  for _____ 's halftime show _____ -slip.
CELEBRITY   PART OF THE BODY

From ADULT MAD LIBS*: Pigskin Party Mad Libs • Copyright © 2013 by Penguin Random House LLC.

MAD LIBS® is fun to play with friends, but you can also play it by yourself! To begin with, DO NOT look at the story on the page below. Fill in the blanks on this page with the words called for. Then, using the words you have selected, fill in the blank spaces in the story. Now you've created your own hilarious MAD LIBS® game!

NOUN _____

PLURAL NOUN _____

VEHICLE (PLURAL) _____

ADJECTIVE _____

ADJECTIVE _____

ADJECTIVE _____

VERB _____

ADJECTIVE _____

PLURAL NOUN _____

ADJECTIVE _____

ADJECTIVE _____

PLURAL NOUN _____

COLOR _____

VERB ENDING IN "ING" _____

TYPE OF LIQUID _____

ADJECTIVE _____

PLURAL NOUN _____

NOUN _____

NOUN _____

In the United States, a tailgate party is a social gathering held

around the tailgate of a/an _____ . Even _____
                              NOUN   PLURAL NOUN

without tailgates on their _____ still tailgate! The most
                           VEHICLE (PLURAL)

_____ time to tailgate is before a football game, but some
ADJECTIVE

_____ people will tailgate before any event—even a wedding
ADJECTIVE

or a kids' soccer game! The most _____ type of food to
                                 ADJECTIVE

serve at a tailgate party is anything you can _____ on
                                              VERB

the grill. Hamburgers and hot dogs are the most _____ ,
                                                ADJECTIVE

but you might want to make some veggie _____ for your
                                       PLURAL NOUN

_____ vegetarian friends as well. Of course, the best part
ADJECTIVE

of any _____ tailgate is the drinks! Make sure to bring
       ADJECTIVE

plenty of cases of _____ to drink—and don't forget your
                   PLURAL NOUN

_____ Solo cups! You'll need them for _____—and
COLOR   VERB ENDING IN "ING"

for games of _____ pong! Try not to get too _____
             TYPE OF LIQUID   ADJECTIVE

that you can't make it into the game. Or do what the experienced

_____ do—bring your own _____ set to watch the
PLURAL NOUN   NOUN

game from the comfort of your own _____ !
                                  NOUN

From ADULT MAD LIBS®: Pigskin Party Mad Libs • Copyright © 2013 by Penguin Random House LLC.

MAD LIBS® is fun to play with friends, but you can also play it by yourself! To begin with, DO NOT look at the story on the page below. Fill in the blanks on this page with the words called for. Then, using the words you have selected, fill in the blank spaces in the story. Now you've created your own hilarious MAD LIBS® game!

NUMBER _____

NOUN _____

NUMBER _____

PLURAL NOUN _____

ADJECTIVE _____

NOUN _____

ADJECTIVE _____

PERSON IN ROOM _____

NOUN _____

PERSON IN ROOM _____

NOUN _____

LETTER OF THE ALPHABET _____

VERB (PAST TENSE) _____

PART OF THE BODY _____

NOUN _____

NOUN _____

NOUN _____

ADJECTIVE _____

PLURAL NOUN _____

PERSON IN ROOM _____

During every Super Bowl, _____ minutes are spent between the
                          NUMBER

first and second halves of the game for a halftime show _____.
                                                              NOUN

_____ years ago, halftime show _____ consisted of
   NUMBER   PLURAL NOUN

marching bands, but now popular bands and artists perform in a/an

_____ , over-the- _____ spectacle! Here are some of the
  ADJECTIVE   NOUN

most _____ performances throughout the years:
       ADJECTIVE

- _____ Jackson performed at Super Bowl XXVII. It was
    PERSON IN ROOM

  the first time only one _____ performed at halftime.
                              NOUN

- _____ Spears, Aerosmith, and _____ band
    PERSON IN ROOM   NOUN

  _____*Sync _____ out at Super Bowl XXXV.
  LETTER OF THE ALPHABET   VERB (PAST TENSE)

- Tom Petty and the _____-breakers performed classics
                       PART OF THE BODY

  like "American _____" and "Runnin' Down a/an
                     NOUN

  _____" at Super Bowl XLII.
       NOUN

- Madonna was the star of Super Bowl XLVI's half- _____
                                                      NOUN

  show. It was the most _____ performance in history—
                            ADJECTIVE

  more _____ watched _____'s performance than
         PLURAL NOUN   PERSON IN ROOM

  the Super Bowl itself!

From ADULT MAD LIBS®: Pigskin Party Mad Libs • Copyright © 2013 by Penguin Random House LLC.

Adult MAD LiBS
GLORY DAYS

The world's greatest *tailgate* game

MAD LIBS® is fun to play with friends, but you can also play it by yourself! To begin with, DO NOT look at the story on the page below. Fill in the blanks on this page with the words called for. Then, using the words you have selected, fill in the blank spaces in the story. Now you've created your own hilarious MAD LIBS® game!

ADJECTIVE _____

PART OF THE BODY _____

ADJECTIVE _____

NOUN _____

PLURAL NOUN _____

NOUN _____

NUMBER _____

NOUN _____

NOUN _____

ADJECTIVE _____

PART OF THE BODY _____

ADJECTIVE _____

NUMBER _____

TYPE OF LIQUID _____

NOUN _____

NOUN _____

NOUN _____

A PLACE _____

ADJECTIVE _____

PART OF THE BODY (PLURAL) _____

Were your days of playing football the most _____ time
                                              ADJECTIVE

of your life? Does watching football on TV bring a tear to your

_____? Don't worry! It's perfectly _____ for a
PART OF THE BODY   ADJECTIVE

middle-aged _____ to want to relive his glory _____
            NOUN   PLURAL NOUN

on the gridiron. Let's take a trip down _____ lane, shall we?
                                        NOUN

Remember when . . .

- You spent _____ hours practicing your football spiral
            NUMBER

  using nothing but an old _____ hanging on a rope?
                           NOUN

- You earned your first-ever varsity _____?
                                     NOUN

- You scored the winning touchdown at the _____ game—
                                          ADJECTIVE

  and the _____ of the most _____ cheerleader?
          PART OF THE BODY   ADJECTIVE

- You could eat _____ pizzas and drink a gallon of
                NUMBER

  _____—and never gain a/an _____?
  TYPE OF LIQUID   NOUN

You big _____! Dry your tears, dig out your old
        NOUN

letterman _____ from (the) _____, and give that
          NOUN   A PLACE

_____ cheerleader a big kiss on the _____—you
ADJECTIVE   PART OF THE BODY (PLURAL)

married her, after all!

From ADULT MAD LIBS®: Pigskin Party Mad Libs • Copyright © 2013 by Penguin Random House LLC.

MAD LIBS® is fun to play with friends, but you can also play it by yourself! To begin with, DO NOT look at the story on the page below. Fill in the blanks on this page with the words called for. Then, using the words you have selected, fill in the blank spaces in the story. Now you've created your own hilarious MAD LIBS® game!

NOUN _____

ADJECTIVE _____

NOUN _____

NOUN _____

ADVERB _____

NOUN _____

PERSON IN ROOM _____

NOUN _____

ADJECTIVE _____

ADVERB _____

NOUN _____

A PLACE _____

TYPE OF FOOD _____

ADJECTIVE _____

TYPE OF FOOD _____

PART OF THE BODY _____

NOUN _____

PLURAL NOUN _____

LETTER OF THE ALPHABET _____

The Bowl Championship Series is the unofficial _____ for
                                                      NOUN
NCAA football. It decides who is the most _____ college
                                                  ADJECTIVE
football _____ in the country. Which one is your favorite?
              NOUN

Sugar Bowl: This _____ has been played _____
                            NOUN   ADVERB
since January 1, 1935, making it the second-oldest _____
                                                          NOUN
game. It takes place at the _____-Benz Superdome in New
                              PERSON IN ROOM
Orleans, Louisiana.

Rose Bowl: The Rose Bowl is nicknamed "the _____ of them
                                                     NOUN
all" because it's the oldest and most _____ bowl game. The
                                            ADJECTIVE
game is played _____ on New Year's _____ in (the)
                     ADVERB   NOUN
_____, California.
   A PLACE

Orange Bowl: The _____ Bowl takes place in _____
                         TYPE OF FOOD   ADJECTIVE
Miami Gardens, Florida. Its mascot is a/an _____ with a
                                                 TYPE OF FOOD
smile on its _____.
                PART OF THE BODY

Fiesta Bowl: This _____ game is sponsored by the
                            NOUN
_____ and salsa company Tostitos. It became a part of the
   PLURAL NOUN
BC-_____ in 2007.
     LETTER OF THE ALPHABET

From ADULT MAD LIBS®: Pigskin Party Mad Libs • Copyright © 2013 by Penguin Random House LLC.

Adult
MAD LIBS®

The world's greatest *tailgate* game

Flip, Sip, or Mad Libs

by Jay Perrone & Walter Burns

MAD LIBS® is a game for people who don't like games! It can be played by one, two, three, four, or forty.

• RIDICULOUSLY SIMPLE DIRECTIONS

In this book, you'll find stories containing blank spaces where words are left out. One player, the READER, selects one of the stories. The READER shouldn't tell anyone what the story is about. Instead, the READER should ask the other players, the WRITERS, to give words to fill in the blank spaces in the story.

• TO PLAY

The READER asks each WRITER in turn to call out words—adjectives or nouns or whatever the spaces call for—and uses them to fill in the blank spaces in the story. The result is your very own MAD LIBS®! Then, when the READER reads the completed MAD LIBS® to the other players, they will discover they have written a story that is fantastic, screamingly funny, shocking, silly, crazy, or just plain dumb—depending on the words each WRITER called out.

• EXAMPLE (*Before* and *After*)

" _____ !" he said _____
       EXCLAMATION   ADVERB

as he jumped into his convertible _____ and
                                                           NOUN

drove off with his _____ wife.
                              ADJECTIVE

" _____*Ouch*_____ !" he said _____*stupidly*_____
       EXCLAMATION   ADVERB

as he jumped into his convertible _____*cat*_____ and
                                                           NOUN

drove off with his _____*brave*_____ wife.
                              ADJECTIVE

In case you have forgotten what adjectives, adverbs, nouns, and verbs are, here is a quick review:

An **ADJECTIVE** describes something or somebody. *Lumpy*, *soft*, *ugly*, *messy*, and *short* are adjectives.

An **ADVERB** tells how something is done. It modifies a verb and usually ends in "ly." *Modestly*, *stupidly*, *greedily*, and *carefully* are adverbs.

A **NOUN** is the name of a person, place, or thing. *Sidewalk*, *umbrella*, *bridle*, *bathtub*, and *nose* are nouns.

A **VERB** is an action word. *Run*, *pitch*, *jump*, and *swim* are verbs. Put the verbs in past tense if the directions say **PAST TENSE**. *Ran*, *pitched*, *jumped*, and *swam* are verbs in the past tense.

When we ask for **A PLACE**, we mean any sort of place: a country or city (*Spain*, *Cleveland*) or a room (*bathroom*, *kitchen*).

An **EXCLAMATION** or **SILLY WORD** is any sort of funny sound, gasp, grunt, or outcry, like *Wow!*, *Ouch!*, *Whomp!*, *Ick!*, and *Gadzooks!*

When we ask for specific words, like a **NUMBER**, a **COLOR**, an **ANIMAL**, or a **PART OF THE BODY**, we mean a word that is one of those things, like *seven*, *blue*, *horse*, or *head*.

When we ask for a **PLURAL**, it means more than one. For example, *cat* pluralized is *cats*.

Adult MAD LiBS®

THE RULES OF BEIRUT

The world's greatest *tailgate* game

MAD LIBS® is fun to play with friends, but you can also play it by yourself! To begin with, DO NOT look at the story on the page below. Fill in the blanks on this page with the words called for. Then, using the words you have selected, fill in the blank spaces in the story. Now you've created your own hilarious MAD LIBS® game!

NOUN _____

ADJECTIVE _____

PLURAL NOUN _____

ADJECTIVE _____

VERB ENDING IN "ING" _____

NUMBER _____

TYPE OF LIQUID _____

NOUN _____

NOUN _____

ADJECTIVE _____

NOUN _____

COLOR _____

NOUN _____

VERB ENDING IN "ING" _____

NUMBER _____

ADJECTIVE _____

PART OF THE BODY (PLURAL) _____

ADJECTIVE _____

Beirut, or _____ pong, is a game of _____ skill and
                NOUN   ADJECTIVE

sneaky _____, usually played by _____ college
              PLURAL NOUN   ADJECTIVE

students who spend most of their time _____ anyway.
                                         VERB ENDING IN "ING"

The game starts with _____ cups full of _____,
                          NUMBER   TYPE OF LIQUID

arranged like a pyramid. The goal is to toss a/an _____
                                                        NOUN

into one of the cups, requiring the opponent to drink whatever

is in that cup. People usually play this game at _____ parties,
                                                      NOUN

which can tend to get _____ as soon as the _____
                          ADJECTIVE   NOUN

gets tapped. The game is most often played with _____
                                                      COLOR

Solo cups, but can really be enjoyed with any type of _____.
                                                            NOUN

Just be careful of the other team _____ the ball into
                                      VERB ENDING IN "ING"

your cup, since you'll have to drink _____ times if they
                                         NUMBER

make it. A lot of _____ girls try to distract players by showing
                      ADJECTIVE

off their _____, which can be particularly effective against
              PART OF THE BODY (PLURAL)

_____ players.
   ADJECTIVE

From ADULT MAD LIBS®: Flip, Sip, or Mad Libs • Copyright © 2013 by Penguin Random House LLC.

The world's greatest _tailgate_ game

MAD LIBS® is fun to play with friends, but you can also play it by yourself! To begin with, DO NOT look at the story on the page below. Fill in the blanks on this page with the words called for. Then, using the words you have selected, fill in the blank spaces in the story. Now you've created your own hilarious MAD LIBS® game!

VERB _____

NUMBER _____

NOUN _____

NOUN _____

TYPE OF LIQUID _____

ADJECTIVE _____

VERB _____

VERB _____

ADVERB _____

PLURAL NOUN _____

VERB _____

ARTICLE OF CLOTHING (PLURAL) _____

VERB ENDING IN "ING" _____

PART OF THE BODY (PLURAL) _____

ADJECTIVE _____

ADJECTIVE _____

VERB _____

In life, sometimes it's easier to _____ up when you are
                                                   VERB

about to lose. After all, if there is a/an _____
                                                      NUMBER

percent chance of success, why not throw in the _____
                                                            NOUN

and call it a/an _____? When throwing a party that
                            NOUN

involves _____ pong, you, as the _____ host,
                      TYPE OF LIQUID   ADJECTIVE

may want to institute a house rule to _____ things up:
                                                VERB

the Panty Run Rule. What is that, you _____? If one
                                             VERB

team is playing _____ and cannot sink any _____,
                      ADVERB   PLURAL NOUN

they must _____ down to their _____ and run
                      VERB   ARTICLE OF CLOTHING (PLURAL)

in public to a chosen destination and back. This gives an incentive

for the _____ team to keep playing, even in the
                      VERB ENDING IN "ING"

_____ of defeat. To make it more _____, make
      PART OF THE BODY (PLURAL)   ADJECTIVE

the destination embarrassing, like a/an _____ school,
                                              ADJECTIVE

a church, or a/an _____-through window!
                      VERB

From ADULT MAD LIBS®: Flip, Sip, or Mad Libs • Copyright © 2013 by Penguin Random House LLC.

THE BORING-PARTY GAME

The world's greatest *tailgate* game

MAD LIBS® is fun to play with friends, but you can also play it by yourself! To begin with, DO NOT look at the story on the page below. Fill in the blanks on this page with the words called for. Then, using the words you have selected, fill in the blank spaces in the story. Now you've created your own hilarious MAD LIBS® game!

ADJECTIVE _____

ADJECTIVE _____

ADJECTIVE _____

ADJECTIVE _____

NOUN _____

TYPE OF LIQUID _____

VERB ENDING IN "ING" _____

ARTICLE OF CLOTHING (PLURAL) _____

PART OF THE BODY _____

PERSON IN ROOM _____

ADJECTIVE _____

TYPE OF FOOD _____

VERB _____

VERB _____

NUMBER _____

The world's greatest *tailgate* game

If you ever find yourself at a/an _____ party, find a friend

ADJECTIVE

and play the game "drink when . . ." It's simple—just come up with

your own _____ set of rules! Here are some examples:

ADJECTIVE

- _____ Rule Alert: Anytime someone at the party drinks,

ADJECTIVE

  take a/an _____ drink.

ADJECTIVE

- Drink once if a/an _____ offers you _____,

NOUN   TYPE OF LIQUID

  drink twice if it's the same thing you're already _____.

VERB ENDING IN "ING"

- Count the number of ugly _____ in the room, then

ARTICLE OF CLOTHING (PLURAL)

  drop to one knee and drink for that many seconds.

- If you see a person's _____, take a shot.

PART OF THE BODY

- When _____ tries to pick up someone who is very

PERSON IN ROOM

  _____, have whatever he is drinking.

ADJECTIVE

- Open the refrigerator. If there's any _____, leave your

TYPE OF FOOD

  drink in its place and _____ the rest of the food.

VERB

- Can you get someone at the party to _____ through

VERB

  a/an _____-foot beer funnel? If yes, everybody else takes

NUMBER

  a big drink!

From ADULT MAD LIBS®: Flip, Sip, or Mad Libs • Copyright © 2013 by Penguin Random House LLC.

MAD LIBS® is fun to play with friends, but you can also play it by yourself! To begin with, DO NOT look at the story on the page below. Fill in the blanks on this page with the words called for. Then, using the words you have selected, fill in the blank spaces in the story. Now you've created your own hilarious MAD LIBS® game!

PERSON IN ROOM _____

TYPE OF LIQUID _____

VERB _____

PLURAL NOUN _____

NOUN _____

VERB ENDING IN "ING" _____

NOUN _____

VERB _____

ADJECTIVE _____

ADVERB _____

VERB _____

NUMBER _____

ADVERB _____

NOUN _____

VERB (PAST TENSE) _____

I learned an amazing new drinking game last night! We were at

_____'s apartment. He had some _____, so we
PERSON IN ROOM   TYPE OF LIQUID

decided to play _____ the Dealer. Basically, you take a deck of
                        VERB

_____ and everyone sits in a/an _____ and is given
PLURAL NOUN   NOUN

one card. The dealer is whoever winds up _____ the lowest
                                          VERB ENDING IN "ING"

card. Going counterclockwise from the dealer, each player guesses the

value of the top card in the _____. If the player is correct
                                    NOUN

on the first try, the dealer has to _____ the number of sips
                                            VERB

of the value of the card. If the player is wrong, the dealer says either

"_____" or "lower." If a player guesses _____ on the
    ADJECTIVE   ADVERB

second try, the dealer has to drink for half the value of the two cards

used. If he's wrong a second time, the player must _____
                                                           VERB

the difference between the two cards. So in the case of a three and

a jack, the player drinks for _____ seconds before moving
                                    NUMBER

to the next player. If three players in a row guess _____,
                                                           ADVERB

the dealer passes the _____ and there is a new dealer. I was
                              NOUN

the dealer last night, and trust me, I got _____ really hard.
                                            VERB (PAST TENSE)

From ADULT MAD LIBS®: Flip, Sip, or Mad Libs • Copyright © 2013 by Penguin Random House LLC.

MAD LIBS

A PRE-KEG PARTY BLUNDER

The world's greatest *tailgate* game

MAD LIBS® is fun to play with friends, but you can also play it by yourself! To begin with, DO NOT look at the story on the page below. Fill in the blanks on this page with the words called for. Then, using the words you have selected, fill in the blank spaces in the story. Now you've created your own hilarious MAD LIBS® game!

VERB _____

VERB ENDING IN "ING" _____

PLURAL NOUN _____

ADJECTIVE _____

NOUN _____

COLOR _____

PLURAL NOUN _____

NUMBER _____

TYPE OF LIQUID _____

ADJECTIVE _____

NOUN _____

ADVERB _____

SILLY WORD _____

PART OF THE BODY _____

EXCLAMATION _____

VERB _____

ADVERB _____

You: What's up? You ready to _____ tonight?
<u>VERB</u>

Friend: Yeah! What time are you _____ over?
<u>VERB ENDING IN "ING"</u>

You: In a little while. Did you buy all the _____ for
<u>PLURAL NOUN</u>

the party?

Friend: I think so. Let's do a/an _____ rundown.
<u>ADJECTIVE</u>

You: Okay, we need a/an _____ of beer, plenty of _____
<u>NOUN</u> <u>COLOR</u>

Solo cups, some Ping-Pong _____, _____ pizzas,
<u>PLURAL NOUN</u> <u>NUMBER</u>

a couple bottles of _____, and a/an _____ music
<u>TYPE OF LIQUID</u> <u>ADJECTIVE</u>

playlist to keep it going. Oh, and do you have any more of those

_____ brownies? Those were _____ intense!
<u>NOUN</u> <u>ADVERB</u>

Friend: All good!

You: _____ ! How many people replied on _____-book?
<u>SILLY WORD</u> <u>PART OF THE BODY</u>

Friend: Oh, _____ ! I knew I forgot something.
<u>EXCLAMATION</u>

You: Wait . . . you forgot to _____ the invitation!?
<u>VERB</u>

Friend: Wow, this party is going to be _____ boring with
<u>ADVERB</u>

just the two of us, huh?

From ADULT MAD LIBS®: Flip, Sip, or Mad Libs • Copyright © 2013 by Penguin Random House LLC.

MAD LIBS® is fun to play with friends, but you can also play it by yourself! To begin with, DO NOT look at the story on the page below. Fill in the blanks on this page with the words called for. Then, using the words you have selected, fill in the blank spaces in the story. Now you've created your own hilarious MAD LIBS® game!

ADJECTIVE _____

VERB ENDING IN "ING" _____

NOUN _____

TYPE OF LIQUID _____

NOUN _____

VERB _____

VERB _____

ADVERB _____

PART OF THE BODY _____

PLURAL NOUN _____

NOUN _____

VERB _____

VERB _____

NOUN _____

Kings is a popular drinking game among _____ adults, since
                                        ADJECTIVE

it combines drinking, _____ . . . and more drinking. You
                       VERB ENDING IN "ING"

need a deck of cards facedown surrounding a big _____ of
                                                 NOUN

_____. Everyone starts drawing cards. Each _____
TYPE OF LIQUID   NOUN

comes with its own rule. Here's a quick rundown:

Two—to you. _____ one player to drink. It's like a gift!
                 VERB

Three—to me. You choose, you _____! Drink by yourself.
                                  VERB

Four—to the floor. Everyone _____ touches the floor. Last
                                 ADVERB

one drinks.

Five—for the guys. If you have a/an _____ and a pair of
                                        PART OF THE BODY

_____, you're up.
PLURAL NOUN

Six—for the chicks. Ladies, clink your glasses and propose a/an

_____.
NOUN

Seven—to heaven. Last player to _____ their hands toward
                                     VERB

the sky loses.

Eight—pick a date. Make a new friend and _____ with that player.
                                              VERB

Turn the _____ for Part 2!
          NOUN

From ADULT MAD LIBS®: Flip, Sip, or Mad Libs • Copyright © 2013 by Penguin Random House LLC.

MAD LIBS® is fun to play with friends, but you can also play it by yourself! To begin with, DO NOT look at the story on the page below. Fill in the blanks on this page with the words called for. Then, using the words you have selected, fill in the blank spaces in the story. Now you've created your own hilarious MAD LIBS® game!

ADJECTIVE _____

CELEBRITY _____

ADJECTIVE _____

ADJECTIVE _____

ADVERB _____

VERB _____

NOUN _____

NOUN _____

ADJECTIVE _____

NOUN _____

ADJECTIVE _____

VERB _____

ADJECTIVE _____

VERB _____

VERB (PAST TENSE) _____

Nine—bust a rhyme. Test your _____ skills like
ADJECTIVE

_____ . The rhyme continues to each player until someone
CELEBRITY

makes a mistake. That person takes a/an _____ drink!
ADJECTIVE

Ten—categories. Player picks any _____ topic and everyone
ADJECTIVE

_____ says an item from that topic. First person to stall or
ADVERB

_____ takes a drink.
VERB

Jack—make a rule. For example, if anyone says the word

"_____," they have to drink.
NOUN

Queen—questions. Isn't this a great _____ to draw? Isn't
NOUN

it _____ to speak only in questions? First player who doesn't
ADJECTIVE

speak in the form of a/an _____ drinks.
NOUN

King—Remember that _____ cup in the middle?
ADJECTIVE

_____ some beer in it. Player who draws the final king has
VERB

to drink whatever is in the _____ cup!
ADJECTIVE

Ace—waterfall. Everyone drinks. Each player continues to

_____ until the player before them stops. This card can get
VERB

everyone really _____ up!
VERB (PAST TENSE)

From ADULT MAD LIBS®: Flip, Sip, or Mad Libs • Copyright © 2013 by Penguin Random House LLC.

MAD LiBS

A DAY AT THE (BOAT) RACES

The world's greatest *tailgate* game

MAD LIBS® is fun to play with friends, but you can also play it by yourself! To begin with, DO NOT look at the story on the page below. Fill in the blanks on this page with the words called for. Then, using the words you have selected, fill in the blank spaces in the story. Now you've created your own hilarious MAD LIBS® game!

VERB _____

PERSON IN ROOM _____

NOUN _____

ADJECTIVE _____

TYPE OF LIQUID _____

PART OF THE BODY (PLURAL) _____

NUMBER _____

NUMBER _____

VERB ENDING IN "ING" _____

VERB _____

VERB ENDING IN "S" _____

NOUN _____

EXCLAMATION _____

ADJECTIVE _____

VERB _____

ADVERB _____

NOUN _____

ADJECTIVE _____

Adult MAD LiBS

A DAY AT THE (BOAT) RACES

The world's greatest _tailgate_ game

Hanging on the beach with friends and looking to _____ in
VERB

a quick drinking game? Why not a boat race? Here's _____'s
PERSON IN ROOM

Twitter account of a game in progress:

- Chillin' on the sandy _____ before the wedding. The bride
  NOUN

  wants to do a "boat race." #_____OnABeach #BestGameEver
  ADJECTIVE

- I hope we have enough _____! #YouDrinkALot
  TYPE OF LIQUID

- Lined up in two rows, facing the back of each other's _____.
  PART OF THE BODY (PLURAL)

  _____ vs. _____ or however many people you want. I'm
  NUMBER   NUMBER

  last. Love being anchor! #NotAsGoodWhen _____ First
  VERB ENDING IN "ING"

- Going to crush the groom's team. They can't _____ like we can!
  VERB

  The bride & groom start. She _____ her beer & tags her
  VERB ENDING IN "S"

  sister behind her, the _____ of honor. Holy _____!
  NOUN   EXCLAMATION

  #DrinkNTag

- This is so close! It's so _____!
  ADJECTIVE

- My turn! I _____ my beer _____. This dude
  VERB   ADVERB

  doesn't stand a/an _____. Drop my now _____
  NOUN   ADJECTIVE

  beer. Bride's team wins! #TweetingNDrinking #Multitasking

From ADULT MAD LIBS®: Flip, Sip, or Mad Libs • Copyright © 2013 by Penguin Random House LLC.

MAD LIBS® is fun to play with friends, but you can also play it by yourself! To begin with, DO NOT look at the story on the page below. Fill in the blanks on this page with the words called for. Then, using the words you have selected, fill in the blank spaces in the story. Now you've created your own hilarious MAD LIBS® game!

VERB ENDING IN "ING" _____

VERB _____

NOUN _____

PLURAL NOUN _____

ADJECTIVE _____

PART OF THE BODY _____

VERB _____

NOUN _____

NOUN _____

NOUN _____

PART OF THE BODY _____

ADJECTIVE _____

ADVERB _____

VERB _____

ADJECTIVE _____

ADVERB _____

VERB _____

So, you lost today playing flip cup. You kept ＿＿＿＿＿＿ your cup

VERB ENDING IN "ING"

over and over but couldn't quite get it to ＿＿＿＿＿＿. I'm here to

VERB

help. This is the Holy ＿＿＿＿＿＿ of flip-cup cheat sheets. Learn these

NOUN

important ＿＿＿＿＿＿ and you'll be a/an ＿＿＿＿＿＿ expert in no time:

PLURAL NOUN   ADJECTIVE

- First, put your ＿＿＿＿＿＿ on the cup as you wait for your

PART OF THE BODY

  turn. That way, you can quickly ＿＿＿＿＿＿ it and chug.

VERB

- When you finish drinking and set the cup on the ＿＿＿＿＿＿,

NOUN

  leave just a little lip off, maybe one ＿＿＿＿＿＿ or so. Be

NOUN

  careful not to leave too much off, or the cup might rotate like a/an

  ＿＿＿＿＿＿ when you flip.

NOUN

- I like to use one ＿＿＿＿＿＿ for flipping, but that's a/an

PART OF THE BODY

  ＿＿＿＿＿＿ preference.

ADJECTIVE

- ＿＿＿＿＿＿ flick the bottom of the cup with your finger

ADVERB

  in an upward motion. Don't. ＿＿＿＿＿＿. Too. Hard.

VERB

- If it doesn't work the first time, the ＿＿＿＿＿＿ thing you can do

ADJECTIVE

  is panic. ＿＿＿＿＿＿ put the cup back in place and try again.

ADVERB

Oh, and don't forget to ＿＿＿＿＿＿ your technique . . . a lot!

VERB

From ADULT MAD LIBS®: Flip, Sip, or Mad Libs • Copyright © 2013 by Penguin Random House LLC.

The world's greatest *tailgate* game

MAD LIBS® is fun to play with friends, but you can also play it by yourself! To begin with, DO NOT look at the story on the page below. Fill in the blanks on this page with the words called for. Then, using the words you have selected, fill in the blank spaces in the story. Now you've created your own hilarious MAD LIBS® game!

PERSON IN ROOM _____

NUMBER _____

VERB _____

PERSON IN ROOM _____

ADVERB _____

ADJECTIVE _____

ADVERB _____

PART OF THE BODY (PLURAL) _____

PERSON IN ROOM _____

NOUN _____

VERB _____

ARTICLE OF CLOTHING _____

PERSON IN ROOM _____

PART OF THE BODY_____

NUMBER _____

ADJECTIVE _____

ADJECTIVE _____

Patient Name: _____
PERSON IN ROOM

Height: Five feet, _____ inches
NUMBER

Weight: Told us to go _____ ourselves
VERB

Summary: Patient came into ER with _____. Both appeared
PERSON IN ROOM

to be _____ intoxicated. When asked what happened,
ADVERB

patient responded with, "You _____ idiot, I fell!" After
ADJECTIVE

questioning, patient told us that she attempted a keg stand that

went _____ wrong. She placed both _____
ADVERB PART OF THE BODY (PLURAL)

on the top of the keg while _____ lifted her legs into
PERSON IN ROOM

the air. He then put the _____ from the keg in her mouth
NOUN

as she began to _____ quickly. Unfortunately, the tight
VERB

_____ she was wearing caused _____ to lose
ARTICLE OF CLOTHING PERSON IN ROOM

his grip. She fell face-first into the keg and has a giant gash

on her _____, requiring _____ stitches. Patient
PART OF THE BODY NUMBER

was released after she was _____ enough to walk home.
ADJECTIVE

Status: Released. God help her _____ parents.
ADJECTIVE

From ADULT MAD LIBS®: Flip, Sip, or Mad Libs • Copyright © 2013 by Penguin Random House LLC.

MAD LIBS® is fun to play with friends, but you can also play it by yourself! To begin with, DO NOT look at the story on the page below. Fill in the blanks on this page with the words called for. Then, using the words you have selected, fill in the blank spaces in the story. Now you've created your own hilarious MAD LIBS® game!

VERB _____

ADJECTIVE _____

PART OF THE BODY (PLURAL) _____

ADJECTIVE _____

ADJECTIVE _____

COLOR _____

NOUN _____

TYPE OF LIQUID _____

VERB (PAST TENSE) _____

VERB _____

NOUN _____

ADVERB _____

ADJECTIVE _____

Adult MAD LiBS

QUARTERS: THE POOR MAN'S DRINKING GAME

The world's greatest *tailgate* game

You are at a bar with your friends and looking to _____ things
                                                   VERB
up a little bit. After all, the pub is _____ with no one else there,
                                        ADJECTIVE
and let's face it, all you want is to get wasted off your _____.
                                                    PART OF THE BODY (PLURAL)
Why not play the _____ game quarters? There are many
                    ADJECTIVE
variations of this _____ game, but here's our favorite one:
                     ADJECTIVE

1. Place one _____ Solo cup in the middle of the table.
                 COLOR
   Everyone puts their own cup around it to form a/an _____.
                                                          NOUN

2. Everyone must fill their individual cup to the first line with
   _____, then pour however much they want into the main cup.
   TYPE OF LIQUID

3. Bounce a quarter (preferably from the year you were
   _____) into one of the cups. If the quarter goes into your
   VERB (PAST TENSE)
   cup, you get to _____ first!
                      VERB

4. If it goes into any other cup but the main cup, the person who
   the _____ belongs to has to drink. You go again.
        NOUN

5. If it goes into the big cup, everyone drinks. Last person to
   finish has to _____ drink the big cup.
                   ADVERB

6. 6. Give everyone different beers so the big cup is _____!
                                                        ADJECTIVE

MAD LIBS® is fun to play with friends, but you can also play it by yourself! To begin with, DO NOT look at the story on the page below. Fill in the blanks on this page with the words called for. Then, using the words you have selected, fill in the blank spaces in the story. Now you've created your own hilarious MAD LIBS® game!

PART OF THE BODY _____

NOUN _____

ADJECTIVE _____

NOUN _____

NUMBER _____

VERB ENDING IN "ING" _____

NOUN _____

VERB _____

NOUN _____

VERB ENDING IN "ING" _____

VERB ENDING IN "ING" _____

ANIMAL _____

SILLY WORD _____

VERB _____

Player One: _swings his_ _____ _around and around._

PART OF THE BODY

Player Two: Is it a/an _____?!

NOUN

The _____ _buzzer goes off._

ADJECTIVE

Player One: How could you think it was a/an _____? You do

NOUN

know we have to take _____ drinks as a penalty, right?

NUMBER

Player Two: Are you _____ this on me? You looked like a/an

VERB ENDING IN "ING"

_____ up there!

NOUN

Player One: Look, we need one point to _____ "charades,"

VERB

and it's your turn.

Player Two: _looks at the card and smiles. She hits the_ _____

NOUN

and then starts _____ _around the room, pinching her nose,_

VERB ENDING IN "ING"

_____ _behind her, and shaking her head._

VERB ENDING IN "ING"

Player One: Ummm . . . you're "Drunk as a/an _____?"

ANIMAL

Player Two: _____! You got it!

SILLY WORD

The other teams sigh and _____ _their beers._

VERB

From ADULT MAD LIBS®: Flip, Sip, or Mad Libs • Copyright © 2013 by Penguin Random House LLC.

Adult MAD LiBS

POWER HOUR AND THE PLAYLIST

The world's greatest *tailgate* game

MAD LIBS® is fun to play with friends, but you can also play it by yourself! To begin with, DO NOT look at the story on the page below. Fill in the blanks on this page with the words called for. Then, using the words you have selected, fill in the blank spaces in the story. Now you've created your own hilarious MAD LIBS® game!

ADJECTIVE _____

TYPE OF LIQUID _____

NUMBER _____

ADVERB _____

NUMBER _____

COLOR _____

VERB _____

NOUN _____

TYPE OF LIQUID _____

ANIMAL _____

NOUN _____

ADJECTIVE _____

NOUN _____

NOUN _____

ADJECTIVE _____

NOUN _____

VERB ENDING IN "ING" _____

ADVERB _____

If you love music, power hour is the _____ drinking

ADJECTIVE

game for you. Start off with plenty of _____ and some

TYPE OF LIQUID

shot glasses. You can play with as few as two people and as many

as _____ (but we _____ recommend not

NUMBER ADVERB

doing this alone!). The goal is to take a shot every minute for

_____ minutes. To get you started, here is a list of the most

NUMBER

popular power-hour songs:

- "_____ Solo Cup" by Toby Keith

COLOR

- "Why Don't We _____ and Screw" by Jimmy _____

VERB NOUN

- "_____ & Juice" by Snoop _____

TYPE OF LIQUID ANIMAL

- "You & Me & the _____ Makes 3" by _____

NOUN ADJECTIVE

Bad _____ Daddy

NOUN

- "One Bourbon, One Scotch, One _____" by George

NOUN

Thoro-_____

ADJECTIVE

- "Champagne Super-_____" by Oasis

NOUN

Always end with "Don't Stop _____." Everyone will be

VERB ENDING IN "ING"

_____ hammered and singing out of tune.

ADVERB

From ADULT MAD LIBS®: Flip, Sip, or Mad Libs • Copyright © 2013 by Penguin Random House LLC.

MAD LIBS® is fun to play with friends, but you can also play it by yourself! To begin with, DO NOT look at the story on the page below. Fill in the blanks on this page with the words called for. Then, using the words you have selected, fill in the blank spaces in the story. Now you've created your own hilarious MAD LIBS® game!

NUMBER _____

A PLACE _____

TYPE OF LIQUID _____

ADJECTIVE _____

ADJECTIVE _____

TYPE OF LIQUID _____

PART OF THE BODY (PLURAL) _____

ADJECTIVE _____

ADJECTIVE _____

VERB (PAST TENSE) _____

PLURAL NOUN _____

ANIMAL (PLURAL) _____

NUMBER _____

NOUN _____

ADVERB _____

ADJECTIVE _____

PART OF THE BODY _____

_____ years ago, the gladiators of (the) _____ met
      NUMBER   A PLACE

to drink _____ and compete in _____ games to
             TYPE OF LIQUID   ADJECTIVE

decide once and for all who was the best drinker in all the land.

Competitors held _____ barrels of _____ in
                       ADJECTIVE   TYPE OF LIQUID

their _____ and took turns drinking in _____
       PART OF THE BODY (PLURAL)   ADJECTIVE

quantities. After that came the beerathon, in which runners

_____ of foot _____ across fields of _____
   ADJECTIVE   VERB (PAST TENSE)   PLURAL NOUN

holding goblets of beer. They were not allowed to spill even the tiniest

drop, lest they be disqualified and thrown into a pit of bloodthirsty

_____. The events were held every _____ years to
 ANIMAL (PLURAL)   NUMBER

honor the great Beer _____, to whom many virgins were
                          NOUN

sacrificed. All participants _____ gathered at the ending
                                  ADVERB

ceremony, where the high officiant finished the competition with

a/an _____ closing: "Bless us, oh mighty lord of beer, for thou
        ADJECTIVE

hast given us the drink of life and a/an _____ to match it!"
                                            PART OF THE BODY

From ADULT MAD LIBS®: Flip, Sip, or Mad Libs • Copyright © 2013 by Penguin Random House LLC.

MAD LIBS® is fun to play with friends, but you can also play it by yourself! To begin with, DO NOT look at the story on the page below. Fill in the blanks on this page with the words called for. Then, using the words you have selected, fill in the blank spaces in the story. Now you've created your own hilarious MAD LIBS® game!

VERB ENDING IN "ING" _____

ADJECTIVE _____

PERSON IN ROOM _____

ADVERB _____

NOUN _____

VERB (PAST TENSE) _____

ADJECTIVE _____

ADJECTIVE _____

VERB _____

TYPE OF LIQUID _____

CELEBRITY _____

NOUN _____

PART OF THE BODY _____

VERB _____

NOUN _____

NOUN _____

COLOR _____

Adult MAD LiBS

IMPROVE ANY TV SHOW OR MOVIE

The world's greatest *tailgate* game

Are you stuck _____ a/an _____ TV show or

VERB ENDING IN "ING" ADJECTIVE

movie? Did _____ recommend something he thought was

PERSON IN ROOM

"_____ good" and it turns out to be the worst piece of

ADVERB

_____ you've ever _____? Consider this your

NOUN VERB (PAST TENSE)

_____ day because we have the _____ solution:

ADJECTIVE ADJECTIVE

alcohol. That's right. You can _____ the quality of any

VERB

bad TV show or movie with your favorite _____. Does the

TYPE OF LIQUID

main character, played by _____, annoy you every time

CELEBRITY

he/she uses a "catch-_____"? Make everyone do a shot.

NOUN

Too much CGI making your _____ hurt? Go ahead and

PART OF THE BODY

_____ the rest of that beer. By the time you are finished

VERB

with your _____, everything you watch could win an

NOUN

Academy _____ or _____ Globe!

NOUN COLOR

From ADULT MAD LIBS®: Flip, Sip, or Mad Libs • Copyright © 2013 by Penguin Random House LLC.

MAD LIBS® is fun to play with friends, but you can also play it by yourself! To begin with, DO NOT look at the story on the page below. Fill in the blanks on this page with the words called for. Then, using the words you have selected, fill in the blank spaces in the story. Now you've created your own hilarious MAD LIBS® game!

NOUN _____

ADJECTIVE _____

ADJECTIVE _____

ADJECTIVE _____

ADVERB _____

PLURAL NOUN _____

VERB ENDING IN "ING" _____

VERB _____

VERB _____

TYPE OF FOOD _____

ADJECTIVE _____

ADVERB _____

PLURAL NOUN _____

NOUN _____

VERB ENDING IN "ING" _____

ADJECTIVE _____

Hello, fellow _____ traveler! Even in an age of
            NOUN

_____-phones, it can be tough to know which are the
   ADJECTIVE

best countries to get blitzed in. So you're not left high and/or

_____ on the go, here are three of our favorites:
   ADJECTIVE

Belgium: Known for their _____ waffles, Belgium takes
                                 ADJECTIVE

great care in _____ brewing their beer with a wide variety
                   ADVERB

of _____. The country has a long history of monks
    PLURAL NOUN

_____ beer, which they then _____ because there's
VERB ENDING IN "ING"   VERB

not much to do when you're a monk.

Russia: We hope you _____ snow, because there's a lot of
                              VERB

it in this country. That's why Russians drink so much vodka! Made

primarily from _____, vodka is _____ across the world
                  TYPE OF FOOD   ADJECTIVE

because it mixes _____ with almost anything . . . even snow!
                     ADVERB

Scotland: _They can take our_ _____, _but they'll never take our_
                                      PLURAL NOUN

freedom! Scotland is home to a number of _____-famous
                                                  NOUN

distilleries, along with a lot of golf courses. Which makes sense, if you

think about it. _____ scotch makes golf a lot less _____!
                VERB ENDING IN "ING"   ADJECTIVE

From ADULT MAD LIBS®: Flip, Sip, or Mad Libs • Copyright © 2013 by Penguin Random House LLC.

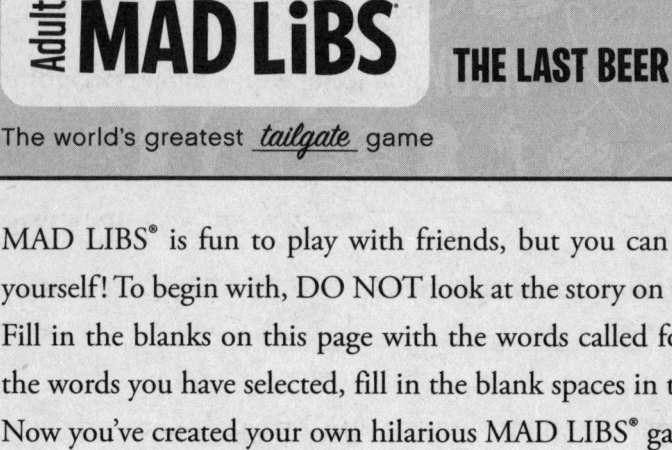

Adult MAD LiBS

THE LAST BEER

The world's greatest *tailgate* game

MAD LIBS® is fun to play with friends, but you can also play it by yourself! To begin with, DO NOT look at the story on the page below. Fill in the blanks on this page with the words called for. Then, using the words you have selected, fill in the blank spaces in the story. Now you've created your own hilarious MAD LIBS® game!

PERSON IN ROOM _____

PERSON IN ROOM _____

ADVERB _____

EXCLAMATION _____

NOUN _____

ADJECTIVE _____

PART OF THE BODY _____

NOUN _____

NOUN _____

SILLY WORD _____

VERB ENDING IN "ING" _____

PLURAL NOUN _____

ADJECTIVE _____

VERB ENDING IN "ING" _____

ADJECTIVE _____

PLURAL NOUN _____

_____ and _____ finished off the last of their
<small>PERSON IN ROOM</small> <small>PERSON IN ROOM</small>

beers. As they _____ ran to the cooler to grab a fresh
<small>ADVERB</small>

brew, they came to the realization that there was only one beer left!

_____! How to decide who gets the last _____?
<small>EXCLAMATION</small> <small>NOUN</small>

How else—a/an _____-fashioned sword fight! They
<small>ADJECTIVE</small>

each grabbed the beer with one _____, and with the
<small>PART OF THE BODY</small>

other, the nearest _____. "En garde!" he said. "Yield,
<small>NOUN</small>

you _____-bag!" she yelled back. "_____!" he
<small>NOUN</small> <small>SILLY WORD</small>

hollered as he charged forward, sending her _____ across
<small>VERB ENDING IN "ING"</small>

the room. Both _____ lost their grip on the beer, and it flew
<small>PLURAL NOUN</small>

upward in _____ motion, _____ end over end
<small>ADJECTIVE</small> <small>VERB ENDING IN "ING"</small>

before it hit the floor. Staring at the spilled beer, he said, "Seems

_____, doesn't it? We could have just split it." "Don't worry,"
<small>ADJECTIVE</small>

she replied. "I think we've got a couple of _____ to suck it up
<small>PLURAL NOUN</small>

with."

From ADULT MAD LIBS®: Flip, Sip, or Mad Libs • Copyright © 2013 by Penguin Random House LLC.

MAD LIBS® is fun to play with friends, but you can also play it by yourself! To begin with, DO NOT look at the story on the page below. Fill in the blanks on this page with the words called for. Then, using the words you have selected, fill in the blank spaces in the story. Now you've created your own hilarious MAD LIBS® game!

ADJECTIVE _____

ADVERB _____

ARTICLE OF CLOTHING (PLURAL) _____

PLURAL NOUN _____

VERB _____

ADVERB _____

NOUN _____

ADJECTIVE _____

ADJECTIVE _____

ADVERB _____

ADJECTIVE _____

EXCLAMATION _____

NOUN _____

VERB (PAST TENSE) _____

NOUN _____

EXCLAMATION _____

VERB ENDING IN "ING" _____

The world's greatest _tailgate_ game

We're here live at the _____ Drinks-A-Lot Arena for the
ADJECTIVE

World Series of Bartending's _____-awaited rematch
ADVERB

between Karen and Diane. Hang on to your _____ because
ARTICLE OF CLOTHING (PLURAL)

these two _____ know how to _____ a cocktail.
PLURAL NOUN   VERB

And here we go! Karen _____ juices the fruit to perfection,
ADVERB

then adds a touch of _____ to bring out the _____
NOUN   ADJECTIVE

flavors of the booze. Not to be outdone, here's Diane showing her

stuff with a/an _____ display of alcoholic dexterity! Watch as
ADJECTIVE

she _____ adds secret _____ spices to her concoction.
ADVERB   ADJECTIVE

Let's try one of these, shall we? _____! Karen's tastes exactly
EXCLAMATION

like a peanut butter-and-_____ sandwich!
NOUN

What a close competition! Gosh, I'm pretty _____ right now.
VERB (PAST TENSE)

Now for a/an _____ from our sponsor! What's that? We
NOUN

don't have a sponsor? Then who's paying me for this? _____!
EXCLAMATION

Nobody? What do you mean, "Why am I _____ into this
VERB ENDING IN "ING"

celery stalk?"

Let's call it a tie.

From ADULT MAD LIBS®: Flip, Sip, or Mad Libs • Copyright © 2013 by Penguin Random House LLC.

MAD LiBS

HELPFUL TIPS TO SURVIVE "NEVER HAVE I EVER"

The world's greatest *tailgate* game

MAD LIBS® is fun to play with friends, but you can also play it by yourself! To begin with, DO NOT look at the story on the page below. Fill in the blanks on this page with the words called for. Then, using the words you have selected, fill in the blank spaces in the story. Now you've created your own hilarious MAD LIBS® game!

ADJECTIVE _____

ADJECTIVE _____

ADJECTIVE _____

NOUN _____

ADJECTIVE _____

VERB _____

NOUN _____

ARTICLE OF CLOTHING _____

VERB _____

ADJECTIVE _____

NOUN _____

The world's greatest _tailgate_ game

"Never Have I Ever" is a/an _____ group game in which
ADJECTIVE

each person takes turns saying something he or she hasn't done. It can be

a/an _____ game, so here are some "dos and don'ts" to help you!
ADJECTIVE

DO: Drink any time anything comes up you have done. Honesty is

a/an _____ cornerstone of the game.
ADJECTIVE

DON'T: Admit to any illegal activity that comes up. You never know

who might be a/an _____!
NOUN

DO: Use your turn to find out the _____ tendencies of your
ADJECTIVE

friend's cute coworker.

DON'T: Use your turn to let everyone know about your personal

life. Nobody needs to know that you like to _____ in
VERB

a/an _____-house while wearing a/an _____.
NOUN ARTICLE OF CLOTHING

DO: Remember who seems to be drinking every time. They're

probably pretty fun to _____ with.
VERB

DON'T: Take shots. This game is more _____ when you
ADJECTIVE

have a nice _____ going.
NOUN

DO: Remember: whatever happens in "Never Have I Ever" stays there!

From ADULT MAD LIBS®: Flip, Sip, or Mad Libs • Copyright © 2013 by Penguin Random House LLC.

MAD LIBS® is fun to play with friends, but you can also play it by yourself! To begin with, DO NOT look at the story on the page below. Fill in the blanks on this page with the words called for. Then, using the words you have selected, fill in the blank spaces in the story. Now you've created your own hilarious MAD LIBS® game!

EXCLAMATION _____

PERSON IN ROOM _____

PLURAL NOUN _____

VERB _____

SILLY WORD _____

ADJECTIVE _____

VERB ENDING IN "ING" _____

PLURAL NOUN _____

NOUN _____

ADJECTIVE _____

NOUN _____

VERB _____

VERB ENDING IN "ING" _____

EXCLAMATION _____

PERSON IN ROOM _____

TYPE OF LIQUID _____

ADJECTIVE _____

ANIMAL _____

_____! That hurt. I pity whoever is dating _____.
   EXCLAMATION   PERSON IN ROOM

They clearly have no idea how to handle _____. I mean,
                                            PLURAL NOUN

they volley me so hard that I _____ against the back wall!
                               VERB

Oh, _____, now I have a/an _____ dent. Ow,
      SILLY WORD   ADJECTIVE

ow, I am _____ off the table. These _____ have
        VERB ENDING IN "ING"   PLURAL NOUN

terrible aim. But now I'm headed for the _____ of beer in
                                    NOUN

the corner! Oh, it feels so _____ and refreshing. Must have
                        ADJECTIVE

come straight from a freshly tapped _____. Will someone
                                 NOUN

_____ me off? It's so cold and I am _____ to death!
   VERB   VERB ENDING IN "ING"

_____! Okay, back to the volley. Hmmm . . . seems as though
   EXCLAMATION

_____ is getting better with every _____ they drink.
   PERSON IN ROOM   TYPE OF LIQUID

Nice return! I'm heading for the cup and—oh no, they smacked me

too hard again! I'm heading toward the wall with _____ force!
                                        ADJECTIVE

Oh, son of a/an _____!!!!!!
               ANIMAL

From ADULT MAD LIBS®: Flip, Sip, or Mad Libs • Copyright © 2013 by Penguin Random House LLC.

MAD LIBS® is fun to play with friends, but you can also play it by yourself! To begin with, DO NOT look at the story on the page below. Fill in the blanks on this page with the words called for. Then, using the words you have selected, fill in the blank spaces in the story. Now you've created your own hilarious MAD LIBS® game!

PERSON IN ROOM _____

NOUN _____

SILLY WORD _____

SAME PERSON IN ROOM _____

ADVERB _____

NUMBER _____

PART OF THE BODY (PLURAL) _____

PERSON IN ROOM _____

NOUN _____

NUMBER _____

VERB _____

VERB ENDING IN "ING" _____

PART OF THE BODY _____

VERB _____

ADVERB _____

TYPE OF LIQUID _____

Adult MAD LiBS® PLEDGE STATUS REPORT

The world's greatest *tailgate* game

Pledge Name: _____
<small>PERSON IN ROOM</small>

Fraternity: _____ Beta Epsilon _____
<small>NOUN</small>   <small>SILLY WORD</small>

Summary: This past weekend, _____, a freshman
<small>SAME PERSON IN ROOM</small>

who shall be henceforth referred to as "Pledge," played Edward

Fortyhands. Goals were _____ explained ahead of time:
<small>ADVERB</small>

duct-tape _____ forties of malt liquor to his _____
<small>NUMBER</small>   <small>PART OF THE BODY (PLURAL)</small>

and consume said beverages within the allotted time frame. Pledge

was only allowed to ask _____ (aka the medic) to hold
<small>PERSON IN ROOM</small>

one of his beverages so that he could use the _____-room.
<small>NOUN</small>

Approximately _____ minutes in, Pledge began to _____
<small>NUMBER</small>   <small>VERB</small>

around the room looking for the medic. Unfortunately for him, she

was _____ yours truly upstairs in the master bedroom, at
<small>VERB ENDING IN "ING"</small>

which point Pledge began asking every female at the party to hold his

_____ so he could _____ in the bathroom. As a result,
<small>PART OF THE BODY</small>   <small>VERB</small>

Pledge was _____ removed from the party.
<small>ADVERB</small>

Disciplinary Action: Pledge must clean the house for the next two

months using only his own _____ and a toothbrush.
<small>TYPE OF LIQUID</small>

From ADULT MAD LIBS®: Flip, Sip, or Mad Libs • Copyright © 2013 by Penguin Random House LLC.

Enjoy more ADULT MAD LIBS®